UNBELIEVABLE!

34 AMAZING FACTS ABOUT DINOSAURS

Hannah Gramson

Lerner Publications ◆ Minneapolis

Lerner Publications Company
An imprint of Lerner Publishing Group, Inc.
241 First Avenue North
Minneapolis, MN 55401 USA

For reading levels and more information, look up this title at www.lernerbooks.com.

Main body text set in ITC Franklin Gothic Std.
Typeface provided by Adobe Systems.

Editor: Elena Mai **Designer:** Mary Ross

Library of Congress Cataloging-in-Publication Data

Names: Gramson, Hannah author
Title: 34 amazing facts about dinosaurs / Hannah Gramson.
Other titles: Thirty four amazing facts about dinosaurs
Description: Minneapolis : Lerner Publications, [2026] | Series: Unbelievable! (Updog books) | Includes bibliographical references and index. | Audience: Ages 8–11 | Audience: Grades 2–3 | Summary: "Dinosaurs roamed Earth for hundreds of millions of years before going extinct. Readers discover fascinating facts about these reptiles' diverse sizes, behaviors, diets, and more in this thrilling book"—Provided by publisher.
Identifiers: LCCN 2025007867 (print) | LCCN 2025007868 (ebook) | ISBN 9798765689721 library binding | ISBN 9798765699546 epub
Subjects: LCSH: Dinosaurs—Miscellanea—Juvenile literature | Paleontology—Miscellanea—Juvenile literature
Classification: LCC QE861.5 .G736 2026 (print) | LCC QE861.5 (ebook) | DDC 567.9—dc23/eng/20250516

LC record available at https://lccn.loc.gov/2025007867
LC ebook record available at https://lccn.loc.gov/2025007868

ISBN 979-8-3480-2948-7 (pbk.)

Manufactured in the United States of America
1-1012511-54840-5/12/2025

Table of Contents

Rulers of Earth 4

Sizing Up the Danger 10

List Break! 16

Dino Diets 18

Strange but True 24

Glossary 30

Check It Out! 31

Index 32

RULERS OF EARTH

Dinosaurs ruled Earth for about 165 million years.

They went extinct about sixty-five million years ago.

Dinosaurs were reptiles.

There were over seven hundred different species of dinosaurs.

Scientists learn about dinosaurs by studying fossils.

The most common fossils are bones and teeth.

Up Next!

BIG AND SMALL.

SIZING UP THE DANGER

An Argentinosaurus could grow up to 131 feet (40 m) long.

That's about as long as four fire trucks.

Sauroposeidon was the tallest dinosaur. It was nearly 60 feet (18 m) tall.

That's taller than three giraffes
stacked on top of one another!

Not all dinosaurs were big.

Compsognathus was one of the smallest dinosaurs. It grew to about the size of a chicken.

LIST BREAK!

Dinosaurs came in all sizes. Here are the top five biggest dinosaurs by length!*

1. Argentinosaurus: 131 feet (40 m)
2. Turiasaurus: 128 feet (39 m)
3. Patagotitan: 122 feet (37.5 m)
4. Sauroposeidon: 111 feet (34 m)
5. Puertasaurus: 98 feet (30 m)

Turiasaurus

*Lengths are estimations based on fossils.

Epidexipteryx

These were the top five smallest dinos.

1. Liaoningosaurus: 13 inches (34 cm)
2. Parvicursor: 15 inches (39 cm)
3. Epidexipteryx: 18 inches (45 cm)
4. Mei long: 21 inches (53 cm)
5. Bambiraptor: 30 inches (76 cm)

Puertasaurus

Up Next!

SNACK TIME.

DINO DIETS

Most dinosaurs only ate plants.

Ankylosaurus

Some swallowed small rocks. The rocks helped grind up the plants in their stomach.

Only about one hundred species of dinosaurs ate meat.

Meat eaters had strong jaws and sharp teeth.

A T. rex had teeth up to 8 inches (20 cm) long.

Meat eaters didn't chew their food. They swallowed chunks whole.

Tyrannosaurus Rex

Up Next!

WEIRD AND WILD.

STRANGE BUT TRUE

Many dinosaurs had feathers. The feathers kept them warm.

Oviraptor

They also used their feathers to catch one another's attention.

Gigantoraptor was one of the largest feathered dinosaurs. It was 16 feet (5 m) tall.

It had one claw at the end of each wing and no teeth.

Citipati

Most dinosaurs with wings couldn't fly.

Instead, they flapped their wings to run faster. Which dinosaur is your favorite?

Velociraptor

Glossary

extinct: no longer existing

fossil: the remains of a living animal or plant from a long time ago

reptile: a scaly animal that crawls on its belly or on small, short legs

species: a group of similar living things

Check It Out!

Britannica Kids: Dinosaur
https://kids.britannica.com/kids/article/dinosaur/353055

Carr, Aaron. *Sauroposeidon*. AV2, 2022.

Kaiser, Brianna. *The Mighty T. Rex*. Lerner Publications, 2022.

Kiddle: Dinosaur Facts for Kids
https://kids.kiddle.co/Dinosaur

National Geographic Kids: Dinosaurs
https://kids.nationalgeographic.com/animals/prehistoric

Ranch, Jeri. *Compsognathus: A First Look*. Lerner Publications, 2024.

Index

Argentinosaurus, 10, 16

Compsognathus, 15

fossils, 8–9

Gigantoraptor, 26–27

Sauroposeidon, 12, 16

T. rex, 22

Photo Acknowledgments

Image credits: Dotted Yeti/Shutterstock, p. 3; Orla/Shutterstock, p. 4; Grant Faint/Getty Images, p. 5; Kevin Schafer/Getty Images, p. 6; Orla/Getty Images, p. 7; benedek/Getty Images, p. 8; BertBeekmans/Getty Images, p. 9; MR1805/Getty Images, pp. 10, 17, 27; AlexSava/Getty Images, p. 11; Corey Ford/Stocktrek Images/Getty Images, p. 12; Simon Landolt/Getty Images, p. 13; Sergey Krasovskiy/Getty Images, pp. 14, 17, 19; Elena Duvernay/Stocktrek Images/Getty Images, p. 15; Nobumichi Tamura/Stocktrek Images/Getty Images, p. 16; MARK GARLICK/SCIENCE PHOTO LIBRARY/Getty Images, p. 18; Yuriy Priymak/Stocktrek Images/Getty Images, p. 20; ROGER HARRIS/SCIENCE PHOTO LIBRARY/Getty Images, pp. 21, 23; Walter Geiersperger/Getty Images, p. 22; SEBASTIAN KAULITZKI/SCIENCE PHOTO LIBRARY/Getty Images, p. 24; Stocktrek Images/Getty Images, pp. 25, 28; Elenarts108/Getty Images, p. 26; libre de droit/Getty Images, p. 29.

Cover: Richard T. Nowitz/Getty Images.